DISCOVERING
THE KINGDOM OF BENIN

AMIE JANE LEAVITT

ROSEN PUBLISHING®

New York

Published in 2014 by The Rosen Publishing Group, Inc.
29 East 21st Street, New York, NY 10010

Library of Congress Cataloging-in-Publication Data

Leavitt, Amie Jane, author.
Discovering the kingdom of Benin/Amie Jane Leavitt.—First edition.
    pages cm.—(Exploring African civilizations)
ISBN 978-1-4777-1884-1 (library binding)
1. Benin (Kingdom—History—Juvenile literature. 2. Benin (Kingdom—Kings and rulers—Juvenile literature. 3. Benin (Kingdom)—Civilization—Juvenile literature.
I. Title. II. Series: Exploring African civilizations.
DT515.9.B37L43 2014
966.9301—dc23

2013023151

Manufactured in the United States of America

CPSIA Compliance Information: Batch #W14YA: For further information, contact Rosen Publishing, New York, New York, at 1-800-237-9932.

A portion of the material in this book has been derived from *The Kingdom of Benin* by Dominique Malaquais.

CONTENTS

INTRODUCTION

Most people have heard of the ancient Egyptians and the advanced civilization they built along the banks of the Nile River. But just as Egypt was famous in eastern Africa, another empire called the Kingdom of Benin was famous in western Africa many centuries later. This dominion—which was located in the tropical rainforest near the Atlantic coast of present-day Nigeria—was founded by the Edo, or Bini, people. Archaeologists have uncovered the remains of settlements from this ancient civilization that date back hundreds of years.

The Edo people were not the only ones who lived in the Kingdom of Benin. Since the empire encompassed such a large area geographically, many other groups of peoples lived within its boundaries, including the Igala, Ijaw, Ishan, Igbo, Itsekiri, and Yoruba peoples. The presence of all these ethnic groups made Benin a culturally rich civilization.

The Kingdom of Benin, which started out as a small community and grew to be a vast empire, was particularly known for its expert farming practices, building skills, and artistic abilities. Within a few centuries, the Kingdom of Benin had grown into a dominant force in the region—a fact that the Portuguese realized when they first visited Africa's Atlantic coast in the 1400s and found a flourishing civilization there. The kingdom's capital was Edo, a city located about 30 miles (48 kilometers) from the coast in the heart of the tropical rainforest. Today, this urban area is called Benin City.

Upon the Europeans' arrival, Benin City was considered one of the greatest cities in the world. A tall earthen wall and a

This head of an oba, or king of Benin, was found at an ancestral shrine. Notice the low beaded collar and cap. Both would have been made out of coral when they adorned the king.

moat 6 miles (10 km) long were constructed around the city to protect the inhabitants from invaders. In the center of the city was the king's grand palace. Four wide avenues that traveled north, south, east, and west extended out from the palace like the spokes on a wheel and connected the king's residence to other parts of the city.

It's estimated that only 8 percent of Benin's population lived in the capital city. Most of the people who lived in this kingdom dwelled in small outlying villages. The villages were linked directly to Benin City through political and economic ties. Villagers sent their taxes (paid in the form of cowrie shells, livestock, and agricultural yields) to the king. They also sent their men to serve as the king's soldiers in times of war.

As the Kingdom of Benin grew in strength politically, it also expanded in size geographically. At the height of the empire's reign, Benin City (Edo) was located near the geographic center of the empire. The Kingdom of Benin stretched more than 100 miles (161 km) north of Benin City. It dipped into the river deltas to the south of present-day Sapele. It extended past the Niger River to the east, and it flanked the Atlantic Ocean to the west. At one point, Lagos—a coastal civilization located 170 miles (274 km) west of Benin City—was part of the Benin Kingdom. Today, Lagos is one of the largest cities in all of Africa.

CHAPTER ONE

Benin: From Village to Empire

As with many centuries-old civilizations without written records, the early history of Benin is a mystery. In order to learn more about this African empire, historians have had to rely on three main sources of information: data gathered by archaeologists; Edo oral history (legends, stories, poems, and songs that have been passed down from one generation to the next); and Benin art and artifacts, namely the famous brass and ivory work of Benin artisans.

Based on the information gathered from these sources, it's believed that nomadic peoples had been hunting and gathering throughout southern Nigeria for centuries. Experts theorize that people began settling down into small communities around 500 BCE. This transition from nomadic to agricultural life most likely correlated with the people's discovery of iron forging and smelting techniques. With these new capabilities, they could make their own farming implements and advanced hunting weaponry. Because of that, they no longer had to travel from place to place looking for plants to eat in the forest or hunting animals with rocks and slings. Instead, they could grow their own crops in their tilled fields and hunt wild game with more precision.

The rise of Benin and its neighboring kingdoms, Yoruba and Dahomey, is largely because of the development of this

This granary is found in the Tata-Somba village, occupied by the Tammari people of Benin. They are harvesters and collectors, as is obvious by the fact that they store their grain in this handmade structure.

metalworking expertise. With the new tools, the people were able to protect their large urban centers, produce larger quantities of food on their farms, and hunt more game to sustain their growing populations.

Settling Down

When people traveled as hunters and gatherers, they usually did so in extended family units. Because of that, it naturally makes sense that when these nomadic people decided to settle down and become farmers, they set up small communities, or settlements, with the same people (usually their extended

METAL GODS

Throughout the history of humankind, many civilizations have given credit to their gods when new technologies were developed. In ancient Greece, Hephaestus was the god of fire, stone masonry, and metalworking. According to Greek legends, it was from Hephaestus that the Greek people had gained their metalworking skills. In classical Hinduism, the people credited the god Visvakarma for bestowing metalworking skills. The Celtic people of Ireland worshipped their god of metalworking, Gofannon, who was deemed responsible for making important weaponry that the people used in battle.

The god of iron and metalworking in Benin—and its neighboring kingdoms of Yoruba and Dahomey—was Ogun. The people of these kingdoms believed that Ogun introduced them to iron forging and smelting technologies. Because of that, Ogun was considered one of the people's most important and influential gods.

families) with whom they had been traveling. Over time, the settlements grew in population until, eventually, they were big enough to be called villages. Historians believe that by the 1100s CE, most of the people in Benin lived in villages.

Family was very important to the early people of Benin. Their religion taught them to treat their elders and ancestors with respect. Thus, when a relative died, he or she was not forgotten. Family members built altars for the departed relative to commemorate the person's life and celebrate his or her important achievements. It was believed that these altars were places where family members could visit and converse with deceased loved ones. The people of Benin believed that their dead ancestors had the ability to protect and watch over those who were still living. Altars were built for commoners and kings alike. However, the higher the wealth and status or social standing of the person, the more elaborate the altar and the artwork associated with it.

Archaeologists have found evidence that by approximately 1100 CE, surrounding villages started merging into what would be similar to today's megalopolises, just on a smaller scale. When one village became overcrowded and its borders started expanding, two villages would be right next to each other without any open space in between. Archaeologists have found an interconnected system of village walls that show how neighboring villages grew into one big city. Eventually, these small cities would become one single state, or kingdom, ruled by a king.

Rulers from on High

Many centuries-old civilizations share the belief that their early rulers were mythological creatures or gods. The Native Americans have legends attesting to that. So do the Greeks, Hindus, Japanese, and Chinese. Many also believed—like the ancient Egyptians—that their kings, queens, emperors, and pharaohs were direct descendants of those gods and were thus destined to become rulers because of their pure "royal blood." Even some monarchies today claim to trace their lineage back to God, thereby giving them the divine authority to rule over human beings.

The people of Benin were no different. They also shared the belief that their early leaders were gods and their current leaders were the offspring of the gods. The first rulers of the Kingdom of Benin were the "sky kings," or Ogiso. It's estimated that there were thirty-one kings who reigned during the Ogiso period. For reasons unknown to historians, the Ogiso were unable to hold onto their kingdom. In approximately 1300 CE, they were ousted from power.

Oba Is Born

When the Ogiso lost power, the assembly of Edo chiefs, or *uzama*, was commissioned to find a new ruler. These chiefs collaborated with the king of neighboring Ife, who sent his son Oranmiyan—a warrior prince believed to be part god and part man—to be Benin's ruler. Oranmiyan married an Edo woman and had a son named Eweke. When Eweke I eventually took power following his father's death, he became the first king to be called *oba*. This same dynasty, the Oranmiyan Dynasty, still rules today. In fact, Oba Erediauwa, the current king, is the thirty-eighth king in this long royal line.

The sole reason that the uzama asked the kingdom of Ife for a ruler was because they wanted their king to be of royal blood. In Benin and in many other cultures around the world today, royal blood equals divinity. The oba was considered to be more than just a man. He was a literal descendant of the gods who seemed to occupy a higher post than "the Pope does in Catholic Europe," according to an eighteenth-century

This head shows an Edo warrior wearing a brass helmet. The helmet was worn during a special dance that was performed in honor of Oranmiyan's father.

European visitor. In 1668, Dr. Olfert Dapper, a Dutch physician and writer, reported about the oba:

> The King shows himself only once a year to his people, going out of his court on horseback, beautifully attired with all sorts of royal ornaments, and accompanied by three or four hundred noblemen on horseback and on foot, and a great number of musicians before and behind him, playing merry tunes on all sorts of musical instruments…Then he does not ride far from the court, but soon returns thither after a little tour. Then the king causes some tame leopards that he keeps for his pleasure to be led about in chains…

Because of these godlike qualities, the people of Benin revered their oba and were willing to follow his dictates. They believed that he had the power to ask favors of the gods and could therefore promote their prosperity and health. In addition to bestowing good things on his people, the oba also had the power to enact destruction upon them by calling for their executions and ordering them into battle. This great royal power encouraged a strong sense of allegiance and obedience among the people toward their oba.

The Oranmiyan Dynasty

Even though the uzama had wanted and requested leadership from the neighboring kingdom of Ife, the chiefs initially seemed to exhibit a sense of resentment at having non-Edo kings ruling them. From Eweka I's reign down to the several kings who reigned after him, there was constant conflict between the hereditary chiefs and the Benin royal palace. The two groups had different ideas about how the kingdom should be run. The kings wanted more power to be held by the royal family, while the uzama wanted to retain the power they had long held before the kings took the throne.

BENIN'S MOST NOTEWORTHY OBAS

Eweka I Came to power around 1300 CE.

Ewedo Ruled in the late-1300s.

Ewuare Ruled in the mid-1400s.

Ozolua Ruled in the late-1400s.

Esigie Ruled in the early-1500s.

Ewuakpe Ruled in the late-1600s.

Akenzua I Ruled in the early-1700s.

Eresonyen Ruled in the mid-1700s.

Ovoranmwen Ruled in the late-1800s. Dethroned by the British.

Eweka II Ruled from 1914 to 1933.

Akenzua II Ruled from 1933 to 1978.

Erediauwa 1978 to present.

Supreme Authority in the Land

In the 1300s, Ewedo—the fourth king in the Oranmiyan dynasty—won a particularly important battle, which secured his control over the central part of the Kingdom of Benin. It was here that he built the kingdom's capital city, Benin City, with a royal palace in the center. Ewedo's battle victory and capital construction gave him more credibility, reverence, and respect throughout the kingdom. He was able to seize more power for himself and his descendants by stripping power from the uzama.

One of the greatest kings in the history of the Benin kingdom is Ewuare. In the mid-1400s, he became the fourth oba in the Oranmiyan dynasty after winning a dispute with his brother over which one of them had the right to the throne. During this fight for succession, much of Ewedo's capital city and palace were destroyed by fire. When Ewuare took power, he promptly began a

Long ago, this plaque decorated the palace of the Benin Obas. Now, the originals of pieces such as this one are found in museums throughout the world.

massive construction project to rebuild the city and the royal residence. Today, many of the building projects completed during his reign are still considered to be among Benin City's most important historical structures.

As king, Ewuare followed Ewedo's precedent in regards to legislation: he added more laws that decreased the authority of the uzama and made the royal family—particularly the king—more powerful. Ewuare's kingship was a defining one in the history of Benin because, from this time onward, no one had more power and authority in Benin than the king. Oba Ewuare also helped set the kingdom of Benin on a path toward great wealth, glory, and military expansion in what would become known as Benin's Golden Age.

CHAPTER TWO

Ewuare Ushers in the Golden Age

King Ewedo may have established the Kingdom of Benin's capital city and built the initial royal residence, but it was Ewuare who turned both into places of great grandeur. He based his improvements on those he had seen during his travels to cities in the neighboring Ife kingdom.

A Magnificent Capital City

Since the king's palace was in the center of the city, it made sense to have roads that radiated out from it. So Ewuare instructed his workers to build new roads that would do just that. These roads were lovely, wide avenues that connected all parts of the city to the palace.

In addition to newly constructed roads, Ewuare built a grand wall around the city. This thick, 24-mile (39-km) wall was meant to protect the inhabitants from intruders. The king also built a smaller wall around the palace to create an inner city. Within the inner city lived the royal family (in the palace) and the king's most trusted advisers, the Eghaevbo n' Ore and Eghaevbo n' Ogbe (in the homes near the palace).

These groups of advisers had specific duties in the kingdom. The ore chiefs were in charge of duties outside of the

Dancing in royal festivals was, and still is, part of Bini culture. This engraving was made based on the description by a European who visited there (Olfer Dapper) in the 1600s.

palace walls. They served as emissaries between the king and his subjects, collected taxes from the people, and recruited them to serve in his army. The ogbe chiefs, on the other hand, were in charge of the details inside the palace walls. They helped the king manage his household and court within the inner city by overseeing the cooks, laundresses, and messengers in the palace. They protected the king's wives and children and made sure that the artists and craftsmen had the materials necessary to complete their projects. The ogbe chiefs also communicated with foreign merchants who wanted to trade with the king and his subjects.

THE KING'S ATTIRE

As in the past, the oba today owns all the red stone and coral beads found in Benin. The only people he allows to wear these adornments are his chiefs and highest advisers. When permission is granted, it's only for that particular individual. When that person dies, the jewelry must be returned to the king.

The king never gives permission for his chiefs and advisers to wear the full set of jewelry, however. Only his royal highness is allowed to wear the intricately designed red stone and coral as a crown, robe, collar, and shoes. In the past, it

This ornament would have been worn around the waist by the oba or one of his royal staff. This piece has a ram's head at the top and dangling bells at the bottom. It is made entirely of brass.

was said that if the king made a proclamation or curse while wearing or holding his sacred red stone jewelry, his edict would most assuredly come true.

The reason that these red stone and coral beads are so significant to Benin is because of a myth. In this myth, Oba Ewuare stole the precious objects from Olokun, the god of the waters. He brought them back to the palace and, by doing so, became the ruler of not only the land but also the waters.

The uzama were not considered the king's trusted advisers, so they did not live within the inner walls of the city close to the palace. In fact, they lived in homes that were several miles to the west of the city. In order to be a chief in the uzama, you had to be born to the right family. However, becoming a chief in the ore or ogbe was not based on heredity. Instead, it required that a person prove himself through competence and worthiness. In other words, a man had to essentially apply for the job and then prove that he was the best candidate for it. This is known as a meritocracy and stands in contrast to the way one gains or inherits power under a hereditary system like an aristocracy. The king set up the government this way to prevent one particular family (with the exception of the royal family) from becoming too powerful in the Benin government and challenging the power of the oba and his heirs.

During coronations and the Igue Festival, a special Bini sword (called an Eben) is swirled aloft during a ceremony. This photo shows the sword ceremony of Okonghae Ogiamwen, which was performed in the palace courtyard.

Ewuare the Great

Ewuare is one of the most beloved obas to have ever reigned in Benin. Because of that, he is often called Ewuare the Great. He is remembered for the improvements and ambitious building projects that he oversaw in the capital city. He is also remembered as the king who secured more power for the royal family and added to the geographic size of Benin through military conquests. Ewuare was not just a great leader politically; he was also a great ruler militarily. He was known as a first-rate soldier and commander who conquered and incorporated land to the east and west into the Benin kingdom.

In addition, Ewuare is credited with having encouraged the growth of Benin's art and culture. He was the one who started the tradition of kings and high chiefs wearing specific red stone and coral jewelry and scarlet-colored wool called *ododo*. The oba and high chiefs also wore special hairstyles in which the entire head was shaved except for a small strip of hair near the forehead. The king had to give permission for a chief to wear this type of hairstyle.

Ewuare instituted several other traditions in Benin, such as the Igue festival, an event that is still held every year. This celebration—dating to 1443—marks the end of one year and heralds the start of another. It is a sacred festival where the people and their chiefs pay homage to the oba and offer gratitude to the gods for sparing their lives and providing them with blessings. It includes special rituals, dancing, prayers, and songs and concludes with an offering of peace leaves to the oba. The best way to visually describe the Igue festival is with the color red. All of the chiefs are adorned in traditional red clothing, feather hats, bracelets, necklaces, and anklets.

CHAPTER THREE

Expanding the Kingdom Through Warfare

E wuare the Great is considered the first warrior king of Benin. He inaugurated the reign of the "warrior kings," which continued from Ewuare's rule through the next several centuries.

Ozolua, Ewuare's son, was the next oba of Benin and a great warrior king in his own right. He ruled from the late 1400s until the early 1500s and is known as "the Conqueror." During this period, he greatly expanded the kingdom of Benin, which now stretched from the Niger River in the east to the city of Lagos in the west.

As more territory was conquered in battle, Ozolua would send one of his sons to rule over the newly acquired domains. This turned out to be a successful strategy in some instances and a failure in others. Just as the original tribespeople of Benin did not initially feel comfortable being ruled by men from the kingdom of Ife, some of the newly conquered people chafed under the rule of Benin and its oba.

Mariners from the sixteenth and seventeenth centuries would have used maps similar to this one when they traveled to the Guinea Coast of Africa.

First Encounters with Europe

It is believed that during King Ozolua's reign, Europeans first arrived in Benin. King John II of Portugal sent sailors to the West Coast of Africa sometime around 1489. One Portuguese sailor noted about these first visits: "The Kingdom of Beny [Benin] is about 80 leagues [240 miles; 386 km] long and 40 [120 miles; 193 km] wide; it is usually at war with its neighbors and takes many captives, whom we buy at twelve or fifteen brass bracelets each, or for copper bracelets which they prize more."

In Benin, even the brass armlets were cast with relief decorations. These were the types of brass work made from melted-down Portuguese manillas, or bracelets, which were traded for slaves.

These brass and copper bracelets, called *manillas*, were of particular importance to the people of Benin because they were melted down and used in their brass artwork. As was indicated in this firsthand account, the Portuguese exchanged these manillas for slaves. It's believed that the kingdom of Benin was the first African kingdom to export slaves to European traders.

Benin's slave trade started with the Portuguese in the late 1400s and grew to include other European trading partners, including Great Britain, France, and the Netherlands. The slave trade continued into the nineteenth century. In the late 1400s, one slave cost between twelve to fifteen brass manillas, as the Portuguese sailor indicated. By 1517, the price had risen to fifty-seven manillas.

GREAT SEA BIRDS

The people of West Africa, particularly those from the Kingdom of Benin, navigated the waterways with great canoes that could seat up to eighty people. These canoes, carved out of tree logs, were operated by use of wooden oars. The Edo people saw ships with sails for the first time when the Portuguese arrived on the scene. The Edo had never seen anything like these ships and thus called them by what they looked like: "Great Sea Birds."

Increased Trade

Ozolua's son Esigie became the next king of Benin. He was also a warrior king; in fact, his reign began with a battle when he fought with his brother for control of the kingdom. It is for this battle and another one with Idah, a powerful rival city-state, that Esigie is best remembered. He is also celebrated for his ability to increase trade relations with the Portuguese. Benin imported cloth, coral beads, and manillas, which were all used to make clothing, furnishings, and ornaments in the royal court. In exchange for these Portuguese goods, the Kingdom of Benin exported ivory, pepper, and specially woven Edo cloth.

Trade between Benin and Portugal greatly increased the wealth of Benin's kingdom. The people attributed this to the oba's link to the spirit world and the gods who reigned there, especially Olokun, the sea deity. Credit was given to this

Bini art often depicted scenes from life in the Kingdom of Benin. This plaque is like a snapshot of the front door of the oba's palace. Standing guard are four Bini soldiers.

particular god because the Portuguese had arrived in Benin—and subsequently conducted their trade—via the sea.

Along with developing an economic relationship with Benin, the Portuguese forged a military relationship. Portuguese soldiers were hired by Benin to serve as mercenaries in Oba Esigie's army. This relationship shows up in Benin brass work from the time period. Many of the plaques from the royal palace show the oba surrounded by long-haired Portuguese sailors and soldiers.

CHAPTER FOUR

The Beginning of the End

In the 1600s, the political situation in Benin began to decline. The royal court and other high officials spent money foolishly. The kingdom diminished geographically as territories were lost. Princes fought against each other as they vied for the throne in a series of battles that eventually led to a gruesome civil war in the early 1700s.

Often, situations in life have to hit rock bottom before they get any better. That is exactly what happened in Benin. By the mid-1700s, things had gotten bad enough that the only place to go was up. Thanks to the efforts of two influential kings, the kingdom finally began to return to its original stature. Oba Akenzua and his son Eresonyen made great efforts to bring about Benin's renewal. They achieved this mainly by establishing new commercial ties with Europe, especially the Netherlands.

This renewal came at an enormous moral, ethical, and human cost, however. Benin's main export was slaves, a trade in human beings that (temporarily) restored the wealth

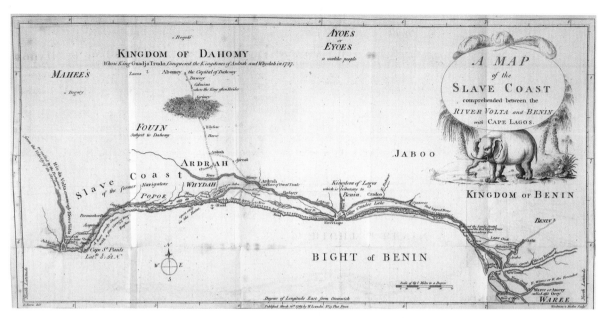

The slave coast of Africa in the 1700s extended between the Volta River in the Kingdom of Benin and Cape Lagos. This map was originally published in *Memoirs of the Reign of Bossa Ahadee, King of Dahomey* in 1789.

and influence of the royal court. The kings who reigned from the late 1700s to mid-1800s were the richest obas ever to rule Benin.

Things again went well for Benin until the mid-1800s, when the kingdom's trade with Europe dramatically decreased within a short period of time. European merchants turned their attention to markets farther south in the Niger Delta. Because of that, Benin lost its coveted position in the trade network between Europe and Africa.

By the late 1800s, Great Britain was Benin's primary trade partner. However, it wasn't smooth sailing between these countries. Trade conflicts between the two nations eventually led to a violent conflict that sadly resulted in the demise of this once-great kingdom.

ARTISTS' GUILDS

Traditionally, to be an artist in Benin, you had to be appointed by the king and be a member of an official association called a guild. Guild membership was strictly monitored and was passed on from father to son.

The brass workers were members of the Igun Eronmwon guild, while the ivory workers were members of the Igbesanmwan guild. It's believed that the brass workers' guild was founded by either King Ewuare or King Esigie. The ivory guild was founded hundreds of years earlier by one of the Ogiso kings. Since most of the guilds' artwork was used by the king inside his royal palace, artists naturally worked within the walls of the king's inner city.

The pieces of art all had different meanings. Some were displayed during ceremonies that honored the king. Others were religious in nature and were designed to honor the gods. These particular pieces were placed on the altars of deceased obas to help them more easily link to the spirit world in the afterlife.

Incurring the Wrath of the British Empire

In 1888, Oba Ovoramwen took the throne. In 1892, he signed an agreement with Great Britain that promised to open up the country to more trade with British merchants. After five years, the British didn't feel that the oba was living up to his end of the bargain.

A British consul named James Phillips, without direction or authority from the British monarchy, sought to converse with the king of Benin. He traveled with about eight British associates and two hundred Africans. Most of the men were unarmed.

When the men arrived in Benin, the country was in the midst of celebrating the Igue festival, so the king at the time, Oba Ovoramwen, asked them to delay their visit. Phillips and

Ovonramwen Nogbaisi, also called Overami, ruled Benin between 1888 and 1914. He is shown here *(center)* with his two queens Egbe *(left)* and Aighobahi *(right)* and two of his children, the Princess Orinmwiame and Prince Uyiekpen.

his men continued onward despite this request. As they traveled toward Benin City, they were ambushed and killed by a group of Edo warriors. This act was apparently not sanctioned by the oba but was ordered by some of the tribal chiefs.

This violent ambush of British citizens set off a domino effect that could not be stopped. Within a few weeks, a British military force of 1,500 men, called the Punitive Expedition, arrived from London and marched toward Benin City. They captured the oba and sent him to live in exile in the neighboring town of Calabar.

Benin's Demise

With the king and his court banished, the royal palace and all its finery were deemed the spoils of war. The palace was decorated with hundreds of pieces of fine artwork, including intricately designed brass plaques, ornate ivory carvings, and detailed brass figurines. The soldiers stripped the palace of all this regalia and took it back to Great Britain.

Oba Ovoramwen lived out his days in exile. When he died in 1914, his son Eweka II was enthroned by permission of the British. Eweke II's powers were nothing like the obas of days gone by. He was no longer the supreme authority in the land. Rather, he himself was subject to the British colonial government.

However, even without this authority, Eweke II was able to restore some of the traditions of the Benin people. He reestablished the state rituals. He instituted the Benin Arts and Crafts School that trained artisans in brass casting, ivory carving, bead working, leatherworking, and weaving. He also reestab-lished the royal guilds.

In the past, the skills of these artisans were only used to make palace-based artwork. But Eweka II changed this sys-tem. He encouraged the artisans to create not only palace-commissioned work but also art goods designed for worldwide clientele and tourists. Because he reinstated the guilds—and the obas who have reigned since him have kept up with this tradition—the country's century-old artistic skills can now live on forever and be appreciated all around the world.

CHAPTER FIVE

Benin's Famous Art

When curators at the British museums saw the art-work brought back from the oba's palace by victorious British forces in 1897, they were stunned at the advanced quality of the work. It was easily as good as anything created by the European Renaissance masters. The curators certainly did not expect this sophisticated artistry to come from Benin. After all, they (along with many Europeans of that time period) considered Africans to be a primitive people incapable of such innovative techniques and art forms.

Thanks to the art of Benin and the artistry of its people, the Western world's view of African nations would forever be changed. Museums and art collectors around the world vied for a chance to purchase the art. Today, the finest museums around the world (the British Museum, the Metropolitan Museum of Art in New York, the Ethnological Museum of Berlin, etc.) have collections of Benin art. It's this artwork that has made the Kingdom of Benin famous worldwide.

Exclusive to the King's Court

Over the centuries, the obas used art for more than just decoration. They used these pieces to tout their political and spiritual

Leopards were very popular animals in Bini art. This piece of jewelry would have been worn as an armband in the oba's ceremonial attire.

power. Every aspect of the artwork was significant. The materials used in the art had particular meanings. For example, if brass was used to create the art, a different meaning was intended than if ivory or red beads were used. The people and animals in the artwork also gave specific meaning to the pieces. Generally, the oba was shown in the artwork. But occasionally other subjects would be depicted as well, such as the oba's mother, high chiefs, Portuguese soldiers and merchants, and many different kinds of animals like leopards and snakes.

ANIMALS IN BENIN ARTWORK

Animals were very important in Benin culture. They often symbolized various deities and the power of the king. Some of the most common animals to appear in Benin artwork include fish (mudfish in particular), snakes, leopards, crocodiles, elephants, birds (bird of prophecy), and fowl (roosters). Here are the symbolic meanings of some of these animals:

- Crocodiles are associated with both Olokun, the god of the waters, and the oba, since he had the power to take human life. These animals were the "police officers" of the waters because, with their ferocity, they were in charge of keeping everyone and everything in line.

- Snakes symbolize Osun, the god of nature, while pythons symbolize Olokun, the god of water. According to Benin religious tradition, snakes are sent to punish those who do evil.

- Leopards are considered the "kings of the bush." Because of these animals' power and authority in the forest, they were most closely associated with the oba, who had supreme command over the Benin people. Some of the obas even had pet leopards that were paraded through the streets on chains. This demonstrated the oba's authority over all creatures, including the king of the forest.

- The mudfish lives in shallow water near riverbanks. Because it dwells in between land and water, it's the perfect symbol for the oba himself, since he is considered a link between the people and the gods. The mudfish symbolizes peace, fertility, and prosperity.

- Roosters symbolize wealth and prosperity. They were often found on artwork associated with the oba and the queen mother.

Ivory Artwork

Ivory is a creamy white substance that is obtained from the tusks of elephants. The elephant symbolizes physical power, wisdom, leadership, and long life—all qualities associated with the oba. So naturally an elephant tusk would be used in artwork associated with the king. If an elephant were hunted in Benin, the oba would always receive one of the two tusks as a tax. Ivory was extremely valuable because it was highly prized by both the royal court and European traders. Ivory symbolized the oba's spiritual power and his political authority and vast wealth.

Carved ivory tusks were used on the altars of dead obas. When a new oba took the throne, he would commission special tusk carvings for the altars of his father and other ancestors. These tusks, which were believed to symbolize the king's link to heaven, would top a brass head that represented the personality and achievements of the deceased obas. When the British seized the art contained within the oba's palace, hundreds of these carved ivory tusks were removed from the altars of the obas and eventually found homes in museums around the world.

Ivory was also used to make fine pendants, masks, hand-held clappers, musical instruments, trumpets, bracelets, and delicate figures of kings and queens. In the 1400s and 1500s, ivory was carved into objects to sell to the Portuguese, including spoons, knife handles, drinking containers, and lidded containers and jewelry boxes. The artists carved images that related more to Portuguese culture than Benin culture, including knights, angels, animals, boats, and European children. This was a completely new kind of art that was tailored specifically to the European customers who purchased them. This tradition continued throughout the 1700s as other European nations began trading with Benin.

Brass Arts

Brass is an alloy of copper and zinc. Along with ivory, it was considered a sacred material in Benin. While ivory is a smooth and creamy-white material, brass is shiny and red-gold in color. Red is an important color in Benin, as already indicated by the king's use of red stones and red cloth ododos. The color represents raging fire and symbolizes how temperamental and powerful both the oba and the sea god Olokun could be.

Brass and copper were mainly obtained from trade with the Portuguese. In fact, the hundreds of plaques and thousands of figurines and brass heads that the British found in the king's palace were mainly made from the manillas traded to the Benin people by the Portuguese.

The brass work of Benin is one of the kingdom's most impressive artistic traditions and legacies. At first, Europeans who visited the kingdom thought the brass objects were carved, but upon closer examination, they realized that they were casts. What that means is that an artist first created the object (plaque, bracelet, head, figurine, etc.) in wax or clay by carving all the details into that soft substance. Then he thoroughly dried the mold and poured molten brass over the mold. Once it had completely cooled, the clay or wax was scraped away and the bronze cast artwork was finished.

The Brass Heads of Oba

In Benin culture, the head is the place where the king's spiritual power is located. According to legend (or, some say, historical accounts), when an oba died, his head was cut off and sent to neighboring Ife so that the craftsmen there could make a brass cast of his head to be placed on the altar of the king. This practice is said to have continued until the 1400s.

At that time, it's believed that the oba asked the brass workers from Ife to visit Benin and teach the Edo artisans the craft. From that time on, the brass workers in Benin made the brass casts themselves. Yet, instead of making exact replicas of the oba's likeness, they made heads that were more abstract in nature and represented various aspects of the king's persona.

Other Types of Brass Heads

Brass heads were not only placed on the altars of deceased obas. They were also found on altars that celebrated warfare and altars that were dedicated to the king's mother.

Trophy heads were the brass heads of enemy rulers. After battle, the oba would instruct his soldiers to decapitate the enemy's rulers. These heads were brought back to the oba's court, and the artists there would make brass casts out of them. The castings were then placed on special altars to remind the people of the kingdom's great achievements in battle. Trophy heads were particularly popular during the reign of the warrior kings.

Edo legends say that Oba Esigie was able to defeat the city-state of Idah (the battle that made him famous in Benin history) because of the help of his mother. To thank her for her assistance, Esigie created a new title for her. He called her Iyoba, which means "queen mother."

From that point onward, the mother of the oba was always given this distinction and treated with a special amount of respect. Brass heads were made in honor of the queen mother. She was one of the only women who ever showed up in the artwork in Benin. The queen mother's likeness wasn't depicted realistically in these brass heads. Rather, her idealized image was shown. She looked like a perfect being with a beautiful, coral-covered headdress and crown.

The mother of Oba Esigie, Idia, was allowed to establish her own palace and ancestral altars after she used her mystic powers to bring victory in Bini wars.

The Palace's Brass Plaques

Rectangular brass plaques covered much of the interior of the oba's palace. The wooden pillars were covered from top to bottom, as were most of the walls. On these plaques were the engraved pictures of battles, animals, religious events, and other special people and times in the kingdom's history. Sometimes they showed the king on horseback (with the king being much larger than the horse). Other times, they showed the Portuguese conversing with tribal chiefs or the king. The artists included even the tiniest, most intricate details, such as styles of dress, shape of faces, costumes, ornaments, hairstyles, musical instruments, and weaponry.

There are estimated to be about nine hundred brass Benin plaques in museums around the world that were seized by the British in the late 1800s.

Figures

The figures in the oba's palace ranged from representations of former obas, groups of chiefs, or Portuguese soldiers to animals such as leopards. Most of the figures were cast out of brass just like the heads and plaques previously described. These three-dimensional images showed the person or animal from all angles. In one figurine at the Metropolitan Museum of Art titled "Court Official with Cross Pendant," the artist showed in great detail every aspect of the individual's attire (from the front, back, and side of the person). This included the patterns on the figure's scarf, tunic, hat, and shoes.

The regalia of the Kingdom of Benin included ornamental masks such as this one from the sixteenth century.

In another piece at the Metropolitan Museum of Art, titled "Seated Portuguese Figure," the artist depicted a Portuguese figure with flowing hair, long beard, and a fifteenth-century style of European dress. A lot can be understood about the era's peoples—both of Benin and of Europe—and their distinct cultures by studying the artwork created by the master Edo craftsmen.

Musical Instruments

The people of Benin used a variety of musical instruments in their special festivals and ceremonies. Handheld clappers were particularly popular. These were often long shafts that were topped with long-beaked birds and were played by striking the bird on its beak. These were made either of cast brass or carved ivory. These particular birds are supposed to symbolize the traditional Benin "bird of prophecy."

As is the case in many other traditional cultures, drums (called *ema olokun*) were an important instrument in Benin. They were used to announce the oba's arrival at significant festivals and celebrations, and they are still used for this purpose today.

The *ukuse* is an instrument played at many palace celebrations, including the coronation of a king. It is similar to the maracas used in Spain and Latin America. The ukuse is meant to summon the attention of the gods.

Bells are another important musical instrument in Benin. They were placed on ancestral altars and were rung to call the people to hear the prayers recited for their ancestors. The

Benin bells are unique in that they are shaped like a four-side pyramid with a clapper inside. The brass-cast bells are decorated in many different ways. Some are decorated with flower motifs. Others feature human faces or animals, such as leopards.

The more elaborate the bells are, the more likely that they were intended for someone who was wealthy or powerful. After all, they would have been the only people who could have afforded such a luxury. One particular bell in the Metropolitan Museum's collection is particularly interesting because it contains the face of a Portuguese man. Obviously, this wouldn't have been intended for a Benin ancestral altar, but perhaps it was a gift to an important Portuguese soldier or dignitary.

CHAPTER SIX

Benin Today

Today, Benin City is the capital of the Edo state, which is in southern Nigeria. It is located approximately 25 miles (40 km) north of the Benin River and 200 miles (322 km) east of Lagos. It is a thriving urban center and is home to more than 1.5 million people.

Benin City has several colleges, including the University of Benin. It's also home to numerous factories, including rubber factories, palm nut oil processing plants, and sawmills. Furniture and carpet making are also important industries in Benin City. As far as agricultural exports are concerned, Benin City (and the Edo state in general) is known for its cocoa, vegetables, cotton, pineapple, mango, cashews, cassava, poultry, snails, goats, fish, and rice.

The city is linked by roads to the cities of Ubiaja, Sapele, Siluko, and Okene. Benin City also has an airport that is serviced by Lufthansa, Air France, and Delta, among many other international carriers. It has major ports on the Niger Delta in the towns of Koko and Sapele.

The total population of the Edo state is about 3.2 million. The major ethnic groups in this province are the Binis, Esan, Afemais, Owans, and Akoko Edos. Most communities in the

Boats sailing along fog-shrouded waterways are still an important mode of travel in Edo today.

Edo state trace their heritage back to the ancient Kingdom of Benin. Because of that, they have similar religious rituals, dances, festivals, arts and crafts, and styles of traditional clothing. The people in the Edo state generally practice one of three main religions: the traditional Edo religion, Islam, and Christianity. The Bini-speaking people constitute 57.54 percent of the Edo population. The Esan account for 17.14 percent; the Afemai, 12.19 percent; the Owan, 7.43 percent; and the Akoko Edo, 5.70 percent.

Visiting Benin and Edo State

There are many beautiful places to visit in Benin City and the surrounding villages in the Edo state.

Benin Moat

The Benin Moat was traditionally called Iya. This deep trench was dug many centuries before modern earth-moving equipment was invented. At 2 miles (3.2 km) long, the moat is believed to be one of the largest human-made earthworks in the world. It rings the perimeter of the city and was meant to be a defensive barrier during times of war to keep the enemy out of the capital. It's believed to have been built in the 1200s by Oba Oguola, with an extension of the moat constructed in the 1600s by Oba Ewuare the Great.

Oba's Palace

Many centuries ago, few people were allowed into the oba's palace. But today, visitors from around the world are often allowed to take tours. This building, situated in the heart of the city, is one of the region's most highly valued structures for its historical, cultural, architectural, and aesthetic importance. Don't expect to see too many authentic pieces of artwork here, though. Remember that the palace art and treasures were carted off by the British in the late 1800s and are now dispersed in museums around the world. The artworks on display today in the palace are only copies of the original pieces.

The Royal Palace in Benin City is one of the most popular places for people to visit.

Igun Street

This thoroughfare is where the bronze casters guild is today. Visitors can stop by the shops and see how the bronze casting is done and browse pieces that are for sale. Most of the casters have been in the "family" business for dozens of generations.

THE UNIVERSITY OF BENIN

The University of Benin was founded in 1970 as an institute of technology. It was given full university status in 1971. Today, there are forty thousand full-time and part-time students who attend the university. It offers a variety of courses in undergraduate, postgraduate, and diploma and certificate studies. Degrees are offered in the fields of agriculture, arts, education, engineering, law, life science, pharmacy, physical science, social science, and medical science. The College of Medical Sciences within the University of Benin has three schools: Basic Medical Sciences, Dentistry and Medicine, and the Institute of Child Health.

Grand Celebrations

Celebrations are extremely important in the Edo community. They are held at various times throughout the year, with some lasting for several months at a time. The two most important are the Igue and Ugie Erha Oba festivals.

The Igue festival honors the king and is held to renew his semi-divine powers. The high point of the festival is when special plant substances are applied to the king's body. These are meant to strengthen him for the coming year. Animals are also sacrificed to give him spiritual power. At the end of the ritual, the king is draped in elaborate cloth. Then he performs a special dance to purify the city.

Ugie Erha Oba is a festival that allows the people of Benin to commemorate their ancestors. It begins with a community celebration during which the ancestors of the oba are honored, especially the king's father. The king dances in this celebration, too. For this festival, he wears his scarlet-red ododo and layers of red stone and coral jewelry. He also oversees the placement of the gifts on his father's altar. The Ugie Erha Oba celebration ends with a mock battle in which the people reenact the reign of Ewuare, and descendants of the uzama fight with the oba. Of course, the oba and his men win the battle (just like they did in Ewuare's time), further demonstrating the oba's ultimate power.

Today's Oba

The currently reigning king of Benin is Oba Erediauwa. He was crowned the thirty-eighth king of Benin on March 23, 1979. *Erediauwa* means "one who has come to put the house or society in order." Oba Erediauwa has worked hard to live up to his name.

Erediauwa graduated with a law degree from Cambridge University in England. Before he ascended to the throne, he worked in several top public service positions in different parts of Nigeria, including Lagos, Ahoada, and Enugu. During the Nigerian Civil War, he participated in the Aburi peace talks.

When he came to power, Erediauwa modernized the palace courtyard. He created positions for many new chiefs to help him meet the various needs of the kingdom. He has been the leader during a very tumultuous period of the area's history that has included several military coups and revolts.

Red is still the color of royalty in Benin. This picture of the late Oba Akenzua II shows the king in his full red and coral regalia.

Under his rule, Erediauwa has fostered a return to the traditional ways of the kingdom. He encourages the celebration of special ceremonies and festivals as a way for his people to truly understand their history and culture. He also encourages education in the traditional arts of the kingdom. Under the reign of Erediauwa, Benin artists and artisans—with their carving, brass work, beadwork, and textile design—have shown the world that the Kingdom of Benin always has been and continues to be a treasury of artistic and cultural expression.

The oba and his palace are still at the heart of the Edo culture and community, even though the Kingdom of Benin is no longer an independent nation. In addition to Nigeria, people who trace their lineage back to the Kingdom of Benin are found in many places throughout the world. Because of this global migration, the influence and culture of the Kingdom of Benin isn't solely concentrated on the western coast of Africa but has been incorporated into many communities and cities around the globe.

The Kingdom of Benin lives on today in its beautiful artwork found in leading international museums. It also endures in the globally dispersed descendants of the Edo, whose culture and traditions greatly enrich the places where their modern-day kin—and heirs to the kingdom—have settled.

TIMELINE

c. 500 CE Nomadic peoples of southern Nigeria learn to forge iron.

c. 1000 Nomadic groups settle in clusters, then in villages.

c. 1300 Eweka becomes oba.

Late 1300s Oba Ewedo claims greater authority over uzama and builds the capital, Edo, and first palace.

Mid-1400s Oba Ewuare establishes the oba's authority over uzama, rebuilds and reorganizes the capital and palace, conquers vast new territories, and introduces new art forms and rituals.

Late 1400s Oba Ozolua conquers new territory; first contact with the Portuguese.

Early 1500s Oba Esigie conquers new territory and establishes strong trade relations with the Portuguese.

Early 1700s Akenzua I rebuilds the formerly declining power of the monarchy and wealth of the kingdom.

Mid-1700s Eresonyen continues growth of royal power and prosperity.

Late 1800s Tension increases with trading partner Great Britain.

1897 British troops invade, loot, and burn the capital; Oba Ovoranmwen is exiled.

1914 Eweka II becomes oba; he rebuilds the palace and restores some royal traditions.

1933 Oba Akenzua II comes to power.

1978 Oba Erediauwa comes to power.

2013 Nigeria is the seventh most populous country in the world. One out of every four Africans is Nigerian.

GLOSSARY

archaeology The scientific study of objects left behind by humans.

city-state A state that is made up of a city and its surrounding territory.

commoner A person who is not of royal or noble rank.

court regalia Emblems or decorations that indicate close association with the palace.

Dahomey A kingdom that neighbored early Benin.

Edo People who form the majority of the Kingdom of Benin's inhabitants; original name of the Kingdom of Benin and of Benin City.

Eghaevbo n'Ogbe An association of titleholders who administered the king's palace and were the king's closest allies.

Eghaevbo n'Ore An association of titleholders who administered Benin's outlying regions.

ema olokun Traditional drums played by the Edo people.

Golden Age The high point in the Benin empire.

guild A professional organization of artists or craftspeople.

Idah The powerful city-state north of Benin City.

Ife The powerful Yoruba kingdom, the birthplace of Oranmiyan, and an important center of culture that greatly influenced the culture of much of southeastern Nigeria.

Igbesanmwan The ivory carvers' guild in Benin City.

Igue An annual festival held to strengthen the king's powers.

Igun Eronmwon The brass workers' guild in Benin City.

iyoba The Edo word for "queen mother."

manilla A horseshoe-shaped brass ingot used as currency by the Portuguese.

Nigeria The modern-day country that contains within its borders the ancient Kingdom of Benin.

oba The Edo word for "king."

ododo The sacred scarlet-colored cloth worn only by the king and his chiefs.

ogbe The Edo word for "palace"; the side of the king's inner city where officials responsible for palace administration lived.

Ogiso Sky kings; the first ruling dynasty in the Edo region.

Olokun The god of the sea, and the source of wealth and children.

Oranmiyan The semi-divine son of the ruler of Ife sent to Benin.

ore The Edo word for "town;" the side of the king's inner city where officials responsible for issues beyond the palace lived.

Osun The god of nature.

Ugie Erha Oba An annual festival held to honor the oba's ancestors and the power of the oba.

ukuse An instrument played at palace celebrations, including the king's coronation, that is similar to Spanish maracas.

uzama The council of Edo chiefs.

Yoruba A kingdom that neighbored early Benin.

FOR MORE INFORMATION

African Cultural Center
P.O. Box 3147
Grand Central Station
New York, NY 10163
Web site: http://www.accenter.org
The African Cultural Center educates the general public
about the diverse cultures in Africa through music,
dance, the arts, and workshops.

African Cultural Exchange
120-35 142nd Street
Jamaica, NY 11436
(917) 862-2864
Web site: http://www.theafricanculturalexchange.org
This nonprofit organization is dedicated to providing cross-
cultural links between North Americans and Africans.

African Studies Association
Rutgers University - Livingston Campus
54 Joyce Kilmer Avenue
Piscataway, NJ 08854-8045
(848) 445-8173
Web site: http://www.africanstudies.org
This organization was established in 1957 and is dedicated
to sharing and disseminating information regarding the
continent, kingdoms, and culture of Africa.

Art Institute of Chicago
111 South Michigan Avenue

Chicago, IL 60603-6404

(312) 443-3600

Web site: http://www.artic.edu

In 2008, the Art Institute of Chicago presented a special exhibit titled "Benin – Kings and Rituals: Court Arts from Nigeria." It has a permanent collection of Benin art and artifacts. Its Web site includes links to recorded lectures held at the institute during the 2008 Benin exhibit.

British Museum

Great Russell Street

London, England WC1B 3DG

Tel: +44 (0)20 7323 8299

Web site: http://www.britishmuseum.org

Permanent collections at the British Museum range from the artifacts and art of ancient Eastern Africa (including Egyptian) and Western Africa (including the Kingdom of Benin) to contemporary pieces from all over the continent.

Metropolitan Museum of Art

1000 Fifth Avenue

New York, NY 10028-0198

(212) 535-7710

Web site: http://www.metmuseum.org

The Met's collection of Benin art ranges from carved ivory tusks to brass figures and heads. Most of the collection was donated to the museum by Klaus G. Perls and the Rockefellers.

West African Museums Programme
3050 Avenue Charles De Gaulle
Ouagadougou, Burkina Faso
Tel: (+226) 50 48 39 66
Web site: http://fr.wamponline.org
This organization assists in the development of private and
    community museums in West Africa.

Web Sites

Due to the changing nature of Internet links, Rosen Publishing
has developed an online list of Web sites related to the subject
of this book. This site is updated regularly. Please use this link
to access the list:

http://www.rosenlinks.com/EAC/Benin

FOR FURTHER READING

Bassani, Ezio. *African Art*. New York, NY: Skira, 2012.

Bewer, Tim. *Lonely Planet West Africa* (Multi Country Travel Guide). Victoria, Australia: Lonely Planet, 2009.

Campbell, John. *Nigeria: Dancing on the Brink* (Council on Foreign Relations Books). Lanham, MD: Rowman & Littlefield, 2011.

Chemeche, George. *The Horse Rider in African Art*. New York, NY: Antique Collectors Club, 2011.

Diouf, Sylviane A. *Kings and Queens of West Africa*. New York, NY: Franklin Watts, 2000.

Eisenhofer, Stefan. *African Art* (Taschen Basic Genre). Los Angeles, CA: Taschen, 2010.

Erediauwa (King of Benin), India. *I Remain, Sir, Your Obedient Servant*. New Delhi: Spectrum Books, 2004.

Falola, Toyin, and Matthew M. Heaton. *A History of Nigeria*. New York, NY: Cambridge University Press, 2008.

Friedman, Mel. *Africa* (True Books). New York, NY: Children's Press, 2009.

Hamilton, Janice. *Nigeria in Pictures*. Minneapolis, MN: Lerner Publications, 2003.

LaGamma, Alisa, and Philippe De Montebello. "Africa: The Art and Power of Benin." *Calliope*, 2005: 15.6.

Lernieux, Diane. *Nigeria – Culture Smart!: The Essential Guide to Customs & Culture*. London, England: Kuperard, 2011.

Locatelli, Francesca, and Paul Nugent. *African Cities: Competing Claims and Urban Spaces*. Leiden, The Netherlands: Hotei Publishing, 2009.

Mooney, Carla. *Amazing Africa Projects You Can Build Yourself*. White River Junction, VT: Nomad Press, 2010.

Nimmons, Fidelia. *Inside a Rainforest Royal Court: Kingdom of Benin* (Vols. 1 and 2). Seattle, WA: CreateSpace, 2013.

Randsborg, Klavs, and Inga Merkyte. *Benin Archaeology: The Ancient Kingdoms* (Centre of World Archaeology). Hoboken, NJ: Wiley-Blackwell, 2011.

Williams, Lizzie. *Nigeria* (Bradt Travel Guide). 3rd ed. Guilford, CT: Bradt Travel Guides, Ltd., 2013.

INDEX

About the Author

Amie Jane Leavitt is an author and researcher who has written more than fifty books for young people; contributed to online and print media; and worked as a consultant, writer, and editor for numerous educational publishing and assessment companies. She graduated from Brigham Young University and has taught all subjects and grade levels in both public and private schools. Her research skills allowed her to locate a variety of sources pertaining to the ancient Kingdom of Benin, which were influential in the final product that is this book. For a listing of Leavitt's current projects and published works, check out her Web site at www.amiejaneleavitt.com.

Photo Credits